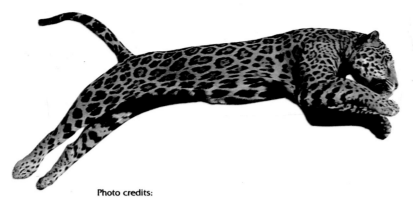

Photo credits:

R.E. Barber — Pages 9, 14, 17
Laura Riley — Pages 9, 12,
Norvia Behling — Pages 10, 26
Tony La Gruth — Page 20
Tim Davis (Davis/Lynn Photography) — Pages 6, 7, 11, 14, 16, 20, 21, 24
Renee Lynn (Davis/Lynn Photography) — Pages 6-8, 13, 14, 16-18
Rita Summers — Pages 6, 8, 14, 22
Charles Summers — Pages 13, 16
Robert Winslow — Pages 6, 10, 11, 13, 22, 23
Erwin and Peggy Bauer — Pages 8, 10, 12-14, 16, 18, 19, 22, 23, 25, 26
Martin Harvey/Wildlife Collection — Pages 8, 12, 14
John Giustina/Wildlife Collection — Pages 9, 18, 28
Vivek R. Sinha/Wildlife Collection — Page 29
Dean Lee/Wildlife Collection — Page 17
Jack Swenson/Wildlife Collection — Page 29
Ron Maratea/International Stock Photos — Page 17
Animals Animals/Samburu G.R.— Page 15
Animals Animals/Gerard Lacz — Page 25
Animals Animals — Front cover
Fred Siskind — Page 29
Kevin Schafer — Pages 20, 24, 25, 28
James Martin— Pages 22, 27

EYES ON NATURE

CATS

Written by
Jane P. Resnick

Hollydale Grade School
Gresham, Oregon

kidsbooks
Incorporated

WHAT IS A CAT ?

There are about three dozen different species of cats, all in the family Felidae. They are diverse in size, from a ten-foot, 600-pound tiger, to the smallest domestic house cat weighing only a few pounds. But all cats (felines) share many of the same characteristics.

Cats are grouped into categories: big cats—the lion, tiger, leopard, and jaguar; and small cats, which include cats in the full range of sizes. The difference between the two is not size but sound—the big cats can roar, the small cannot.

Domestic Burmese kitten

POUNCING PREDATOR

Jaguar

The cat is a jumping, leaping creature able to land on its feet and pinpoint its landing. With lightning quick reflexes, agility, and strength, cats balance in risky places, recover from falls, and spring off the ground. As a leaping, pouncing predator the jaguar is deadly accurate.

COATS OF COLOR

The colors and markings of the cat are its glory. Every coat is individual. The black stripes of the tiger are his own. The spots of the cheetah, leopard, and jaguar are all different. Most coats match their surroundings so that the stealthy, hunting cat will not be heard *or* seen.

Cheetah

NAME THAT CAT

Cats have wonderful names like jaguar, puma, ocelot, cheetah, and lynx. Many of the names were given by people who respected and feared the fierce cats that lived among them. Jaguar comes from the South American Indian name *yaguara*, which means "a beast that kills its prey with one bound."

Cougar

African wild cat

6

Male lion

Bengal tiger

THE BEAUTIFUL BEAST

All cats are carnivores, meat-eaters who hunt for their food. Their bodies are like well-oiled machines with flexible skeletons, strong muscles, excellent eyesight, keen hearing, powerful jaws, and vicious teeth. They are the nearest thing to a perfect stalking, hunting animal in the world. Because of their beauty, secretiveness, and fierceness, cats have always been a symbol of mystery and power to man.

Domestic longhaired calico

HOUSE CAT HISTORY

The sociable domestic cat is the favorite pet of millions of people. Descended from the African wild cat, cats began living with humans in Egypt about 4,000 years ago. They were so valued that the Egyptians considered them sacred and worshipped them in the form of a goddess that had the head of a cat.

The marvel of the house cat is its double nature. A delightful, tame companion, the cat still has the body of a hunter and carries a touch of the wild wherever it lives.

7

FELINE FEATURES

The physical ways of cats are fascinating. No one trait in itself, but a combination of characteristics, enables cats to feed, communicate, and live successfully in many different habitats.

CLEAN MACHINE

Cats groom or clean themselves, and each other, with a built-in scrub brush, a tongue rough as sandpaper. A cat's tongue is covered with tiny, hard spikes—perfect for picking up loose dirt or hair, or rasping the last shreds of meat off a bone.

UNDERCOVER ▲

A cat is a warm-blooded animal with a double-layered fur coat that protects it from wet and cold. The outer layer is made up of long, coarse hairs called guard hairs. The under fur, close to the body, is soft and downy,

The thick fur of these two snow leopards enables them to live on the cold Himalayan mountains of Asia.

SLEEPY HEAD

Catnap is a word invented to describe the way cats sleep— for short periods of time. This ocelot, like all cats, sleeps *often*— about twice as much as other animals.

EAR FULL

Cats, masters of silence in their own movements, are quick to hear the noises that others make. With funnel shaped outer ears and a keen sense of hearing, cats can pick up sounds that are too faint or too high for humans to hear.

African caracal

8

TOUGH TALK ▲

Cats have their own communication system: hissing, spitting, growling, and snarling. Purring, the perfect sound of contentment, is for pleasure.

WHISKER WAYS ▶

A cat's whiskers are not just cute. They are organs of touch almost as sensitive as fingertips. They help a cat avoid objects, judge spaces, and feel its way in the dark.

◀ MINE!

A cat is a territorial creature. It will scratch trees and spray urine to mark its property, so that other cats will keep off. A domestic cat has more civilized ways of marking. It may rub the furniture or a person's legs with the scent glands on its head or at the base of its tail.

9

BUILT TO KILL

To be a cat is to be a hunter. It has been said that every cat is a beast of prey, even the tame ones. And so it is. The house cat who eats from a bowl or stalks birds in the backyard and the mountain lion who bites through the neck of a deer, have the same instincts. Their physical structure makes them excellent killers.

A natural climber, the mountain lion can spring straight up as high as 18 feet, or drop down 60 feet without getting injured.

UNDERCOVER CATS

Most wild cats that live in dense
[gra]ss, brush, or jungle have coats
[that] blend with their surroundings.
[Dap]pled, spotted, or striped, a cat's
[coa]t can make it nearly invisible.
[No]w you see it now you don't—
[an] undercover hunter.

[SN]EAK
[AT]TACK

All good hunters are sneaks,
[an]d cats are the sneakiest.
[Str]ong muscles allow a cat to
[sta]lk and hide, then surprise its
[pr]ey. With enormous muscle
[co]ntrol, this Canadian lynx
[mo]ves ever so slowly towards its
[vic]tim, then freezes. A cat can
[sta]y motionless for half an hour
[or] more—and then pounce on its
[sta]rtled prey.

[TH]E EYES HAVE IT

A cat's eyes are deadly
[hu]nting weapons. Their
[nig]ht vision is amazing—
[six] times greater than that
[of] humans. In the dark,
[th]e pupils of a cat's eyes
[ex]pand to take in more
[lig]ht. These pupils, nearly
[fill]ing the eyes, are strange
[an]d beautiful. But beauty
[is n]ot the point. Detecting
[pre]y is the purpose.

FLEXIBLE FELINES

A cat's spine is so flexible that it can
twist and turn and bound at its prey from
any angle. This lioness
is stretching after
having rested most
of the day.

CAT DRACULA

Canine teeth are for killing,
and a cat's got the best. Cats
use their four dagger-like
canine teeth to bite the back
of an animal's neck. Nerves
at the base of these teeth
guide them between the ver-
tebrae (spine bones) of their
prey. The bite is so accurate
that it cuts the spinal cord
between the bones and the
victim dies instantly.

PAW CLAWS

Claws are a
cat's secret weapon.
Most of the time a
cat's claws stay inside
its paws. During an attack,
a cat automatically whips
out the claws like razor-edged
knives. Afterward, the claws
retract to a relaxed position inside
the paws. The cat returns to its
silent walk, but the claws are
always ready.

The outstretched claws of this
kitten help it to hang on.

11

THE LITTLEST CATS

Care to cuddle a lion cub? Is there anything cuter than a kitten? Cats, wild and tame, give birth and care for their offspring in much the same ways. Except for lions, which live in groups, all young cats are cared for by their mother alone. In the wild, cubs lead a dangerous life and must learn to hunt and fend for themselves before leading independent lives.

Lioness and cubs

HOME BODIES▲

All cats are born blind and helpless and feed only on milk for six to eight weeks. But a young cat grows quickly and, in just a week, may double its body weight. A small cat may be on its own in a few months. But the large cats, like the lion and tiger, mature more slowly, and the cubs may depend on their mother for about two years.

AT HOME AND ON THE RANGE

To feed her cubs, a mother cat has to kill at least three times as much prey as when she lives alone. Smaller cats, like this bobcat, bring rodents and other prey back to the den. Larger cats may take their youngsters along and have them practice their hunting skills.

Clouded leopard cub

PLAYING TO KILL▼

Fighting with each other and stalking small animals for fun are the ways young cats learn to hunt on their own. What is playing today is hunting tomorrow. These snow leopard cubs are learning the survival skills they'll need as adults.

This young cheetah is learning, but the unharmed antelope is evidence that the cheetah needs more practice.

GETTING A GRIP

Children may claim that their parents are a pain in the neck, but not cats. Domestic and wild cats carry their young by the back of the neck—with no pain at all. Loose folds of skin on a kitten's neck are a natural handle. But the lion cub (above, left) would rather hitch a ride on its mother's back.

Lynx kitten

CURIOSITY AND THE CAT

All cats are curious, but kittens and cubs are especially anxious to explore their surroundings. Curiosity, however, sometimes gets cats into trouble. This lynx kitten now has to figure out a way to get down.

LEOPARD

CAT UP A TREE

The leopard is the smallest of the big cats, with an average weight of only 100 pounds. A compact powerhouse, the leopard is the master of surprise attack. The most graceful and sure-footed of all cats, the leopard is the best tree-climber. Secretive and rarely seen, a leopard can sometimes be spotted by its long, elegant tail dangling from a tree.

LETHAL LEAP

How does a leopard hunt? Patiently and silently. The leopard slinks. It creeps. It belly-crawls ever so carefully towards its prey. Then it *strikes* with a lightning fast leap—graceful, precise, and deadly.

TREETOP DINING

A leopard does not invite guests to dinner. In fact, it often drags its kill up a tree to keep it safe. A leopard can climb a tree with a carcass weighing more than 50 pounds clamped in its jaws. The cat stows the victim over a branch, then takes a good rest knowing that its next meal is close by.

DIFFERENT AND THE SAME

A "black panther" is actually a leopard with a coat of almost invisible black spots on a black background. This beautiful dark cat has a savage reputation. But he is no different from other leopards than a blue-eyed person is from a brown-eyed friend.

14

THE SOUND OF SILENCE
Do not listen for a leopard.
There is not much to hear.
The noises a leopard makes are
described as a growl or hiss, a
rasping yowl or even a cough.
It does not roar. Silence seems
to suit the leopard best.

SPOOKY
The snow leopard
oks like the ghost of a
opard. Its thick, woolly
at is a ghostly gray
ith black spots, well
ited for its snowy habi-
t—the highest, coldest
ountains in the world.

15

LIONS

LITTLE LIONS

One to five cubs are born in a lion litter, and they depend on their mother for almost two years. Their playtime is their schooltime. They "stalk" each other and "attack" one another, learning the hunting techniques they must know. When they've grown, the females remain at home, but the males are on their own. They set out to search for their own pride.

A MATTER OF PRIDE ▲

Lions are the only cats that live in groups, called "prides." As many as 40 cats can live in a pride — several lionesses, their cubs and 1 to 4 adult males. They all live together in a distinct territory, which can extend as far as 10 miles in any direction. The lionesses, who are usually all related, inherit the home range, so they must be especially proud of their pride.

GRRRR!

A lion's roar is so power-ful that it can carry for 5 miles. The great GRRR! is an awesome sound, vibrating like thunder over the plains. Lions roar to stake out their neighborhoods, to let everyone know that the territory is theirs. Their roar is like a huge sign: Keep Off! No Trespassing! Or Else!

HUNT CLUB

Lions are the only cats that hunt as a group. They spot prey at a distance and set out with a plan. Surrounding an animal, they drive it toward hidden members waiting to attack. Because they work in groups, lionesses, who do most of the hunting, can easily bring down a wildebeest or zebra and even tackle a giraffe or young elephant—big game even for a big cat.

HUNGRY AS A LION ▼

Lions are not fussy eaters. They eat what they kill, what other predators kill, or animals that just die. And they have no table manners. They snarl and snap at each other, hogging their own portion. They gorge, rather than eat every day. In a single meal, a male lion may eat 80 pounds of meat—and then not eat for a week.

THE KING . . . AND QUEEN . . . OF BEASTS

The lion is known as the King of Beasts for good reason. A male lion can weigh as much as 500 pounds. The female is no less royal at 300. The male, with his magnificent mane, has the look of a monarch. He protects the pride and defends the females against intruders.

SLEEPY HEAD

Lions hunt and eat and . . . sleep. Mostly sleep. It has been said that lions are the laziest animals in Africa. If they've had a good hunt and their bellies are full, lions can spend 18 to 20 hours a day resting or sleeping in the shade.

17

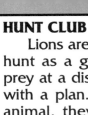

NUMBER ONE RUNNER

The cheetah is the fastest land animal on earth, for short distances. It streaks across the plains at 70 miles an hour. The cheetah's most important hunting weapon is its amazing, deadly sprint. The cheetah runs for its supper and runs for its life.

C H E E T A H

▼ FUNNY FACE

Cheetah cubs are covered with a strange, pale gray fur on their head and back for the first few months. Their faces are funny, too. A cheetah's face is set off by 2 black stripes running from the inner corner of each eye to the mouth. On babies, these lines form an unhappy frown, making cheetah cubs the ugly ducklings of the cat world.

THE ONE AND ONLY

Cheetahs are so unlike other cats that they are a separate species. Their claws do not retract. They do not have powerful jaws. Their canine teeth are not ferocious. They are not strong enough to drag their prey. They cannot roar or climb trees. They do not have long whiskers. They *do* have a deep chest filled with large lungs, and a slender, well-muscled body, built for speed.

18

ROYAL ROBES ▶

The king cheetah wears a royal coat different from the common cheetah. Rare and beautiful, the king has spots that blend into stripes down his back. Having stripes *and* spots makes him a kingly cat indeed.

SPEEDING TO KILL

Faster than a sports car, the cheetah bursts from zero to 40 miles per hour in two seconds. Its claws grip the earth like cleats. Its feet fly, hitting the ground so that, at times, all four feet are airborne. Still running, the cheetah knocks its victim flat, then pounces to kill.

SPRINGY SPINE

The secret to the cheetah's speed is its amazingly flexible spine. When running, the cat arches its back and pulls its feet together. Then, like a spring, its spine uncoils and its legs shoot out, giving the cheetah the longest stride in the cat world.

19

TIGERS

AWESOME CAT

Mystery, courage, fierceness—these are the characteristics of the biggest cat of them all, the tiger. Seven types of tigers roam various parts of Asia. The largest is the Siberian tiger, which can be more than ten feet long and weigh more than 600 pounds. Rarely seen, the tiger hunts alone at night, a silent, powerful creature, beautiful and frightening.

TIGER TOTS

Tiger cubs are born into a world that can be very hard. They may be killed by other animals while their mother is hunting. At 18 months to two years old, they leave their mother to find their own territory. There they will spend most of their life, hunting and living alone.

BEATING THE HEAT

It's hot in the jungle—steamy and sticky. A tiger can't take its fur coat off, but it can *swim*. Among big cats, the tiger is the most likely to cool off in the water.

Splashing, swimming, lounging up to its neck in lakes and rivers, the tiger knows how to get relief from the heat.

TELLTALE STRIPES

People have fingerprints; tigers have stripes. Every tiger has its own pattern of stripes. Tigers' faces are fierce and beautiful, but they are also unique. A tiger's face markings are so distinctive that they can be used to tell two tigers apart.

SHADOWY FIGURES

The tiger's magnificent striped orange-and-black coat is not just decoration. Stripes are the perfect camouflage in tall grasses and forests, where strips of light filter to the ground through dense leaves. Tigers that live in the northern climates are lighter in color to help them hide in the snow.

PALE FACE

A "white" tiger is not a ghost. It is a genuine tiger with a pink nose and charcoal-colored stripes on a white background. Its eyes may be blue—a tiger of a different hue!

THE STEALTH ATTACK

A tiger is not a hunter that chases prey. It creeps up under cover and gets as close as possible. Then it takes a great leap at the victim and strikes with a lethal weapon—the largest canine teeth of any meat-eating land animal. Still, hunting is not easy. Tigers catch only about one out of every 20 animals they go after.

21

COUGAR, LYNX, AND BOBCAT

CATS HOT AND COOL

The cougar, lynx, and bobcat are most commonly found in northern climates, but these cats go their separate ways. The lynx is a creature of the snowbound woods. The bobcat prowls most of North America. But the cougar, also known as the puma, the panther, or the mountain lion, is a cat for all climates. It can be found on cold, high peaks, in steaming jungles, in swamplands, and even in deserts.

TUNED IN

A cat with antennae? The lynx has long, glossy, black "tufts" that stick up from each ear. Like hearing aids, they increase the cat's ability to detect the slightest sound. No creak, or snap, or thump in the forest gets by the listening lynx.

▲ DISAPPEARING SPOTS

Adult cougars have sleek, tawny coats that match their spooky yellow eyes. But cougar cubs are spotted with black. At six months, they begin to lose their spots and become cats of one color.

◀ This Canadian lynx is marking the pine tree with his scent.

◀ A CAT CALLED BOB

A stubby six-inch tail gives the bobcat its name. (To "bob" a tail means to cut it short.) Not a big animal all around, the bobcat weighs about 20 pounds and looks very much like its cousin the lynx.

PHANTOM OF THE FOREST

Bobcats hang out. These cats have favorite places—ledges, tree limbs, and trails—that they come back to again and again. Finding one of these sites may be the only way to lay eyes on a bobcat. These quick-as-a-wink cats are usually seen as fast flashes of fur in the forest.

RACING FOR RABBIT

For mountain cats that live in snow country, the snowshoe hare is a main meal. A swift runner on the biggest rabbit feet around, this hare is still no match for a hungry cat.

KILLER COUGAR

A large male cougar is 200 pounds of muscle. A fierce predator, he can kill a deer with one powerful bite. In his territory, no other animal can challenge him—except a barking dog. The yapping of a poodle sends a cougar up a tree.

23

CATS WITH A SOUTHERN ACCENT

Cats in Central and South America all test the limits of some feline characteristic. The jaguar has incredible power; the ocelot, extraordinary beauty. The jaguarundi is the most un-catlike creature, and the margay is a gymnast that does tricks in tree tops.

SPOTTED BEAUTY

The ocelot has a coat of many colors. Its background fur runs from reddish brown to cream to white. And its spots are a varied lot: solids, circles, and spots that join together to form stripes. The result is a masterpiece of camouflage and one of the most magnificent coats in the cat world.

A hungry jaguar on the prowl.

Margay

CIRCUS CAT
The margay is a trapeze artist, and its high wire is a tree branch. No bigger than a house cat, the margay scampers around trees like a monkey. An acrobat with special equipment, this cat has ankles that rotate way out and big feet and toes designed for gripping.

Jaguarundi

CAT COUPLES
The jaguarundi looks more like a weasel than a cat. It has a long body with legs that seem too short and a head that appears too small. But the jaguarundi male and female find each other attractive and, unlike most other cats, they live together for long periods of time.

ONE FIERCE CAT
Alligators and turtles beware! And monkeys, too! The jaguar plunges into rivers and scrambles up trees to feed its appetite. It dives, it swims, it leaps tall trees with a single bound. When this meat-eater is hungry, no one is safe!

WEATHERMAN
The jaguar is at home just about everywhere — mountains, grasslands, and rain forests. Everywhere it goes, the jaguar proclaims its presence with a roar that makes mountains tremble, grasses shiver, and jungles quiver. Amazon Indians still believe that the roar of the jaguar is the sound of thunder that announces approaching rain.

UNCOMMON CATS

Cats are exotic creatures, magnificent and mysterious, but also strange, and even bizarre. The cat kingdom has some surprising, remarkable, and fascinating felines.

BARE BODY ▶

The sphynx is a domestic cat, and no wonder. Without a hair on its body, it *must* live indoors. It would be hard to survive in the wild without a fur coat.

MOST WANTED

Geoffrey's cat has a distinction no other cat wants. Its fur is the most traded pelt in the world. Prized for its beauty, its exotic coat has black spots and colors ranging from smokey-gray to tawny yellow.

◀ RABBIT EARS

The serval has big ears that look more like they belong on a rabbit than a cat. But these ears serve the serval well. It can hear small animals hidden in grasses and pounce as quick as a ... rabbit.

◀ SLAM DUNK

The caracal can leap into the air and swat a bird to the ground like a basketball player dunking a ball into the net. Its nickname is the "desert lynx" because it lives in dry areas and its ear tufts are similar to those of the lynx.

TAMING THE WILD ▶

The jungle cat is a wild cat known to raid chicken coops. This does not make it a welcome guest in the villages near its habitat. But the jungle cat's kittens can be easily tamed—a reminder that with some cats, at least, the difference between wild and tame can be a fine line.

▲ AQUA CAT

The fishing cat gets its name, of course, from fishing. This cat sits by the water and waits. If a fish comes by, it raises a paw and flips the unsuspecting prey onto the land and eats it. The fishing cat has webbed feet like a duck so it can swim better and hunt where most other cats will not bother —in the water.

SOFT SPOKEN

The clouded leopard is in a class by itself. It is not categorized as a big cat or small cat, but stands alone with the scientific name *neofelis nebulosa,* meaning new cat with a cloudy pelt. It has characteristics of both big and small cats. With especially long canine teeth, this cat has a fierce look but cannot roar. The clouded leopard is a purring cat.

CATS IN DANGER

VANISHED!

Species do vanish. They become extinct, never to be seen again. There are many reasons for this, but one underlying cause is that humans compete with animals for living space. As more people fill the globe, pressure is put on the wildlife that remains. Cats, so powerful in their own domain, lead fragile and endangered lives. Today, they need the help of humans to survive.

PRESERVED WITH CARE

At the beginning of this century, India alone had over 40,000 tigers. By the 1970's there were barely 7,000 wild tigers left. But people began to realize that these magnificent creatures are valuable to mankind. So India and other countries created "preserves," large territories set aside just for animals. Tigers hunt there. Prey is abundant. And people watch their progress with concern and awe.

POISON PREY

Pollution is not just a problem for people. Animals suffer, too. Chemicals that are sprayed on crops to help farmers raise more food, or pollution from factories carried in the air, can seep into the ground and water of the environment. Cats, like the ocelot, who eat small animals can be harmed by the poisons in their prey.

◄ Because of their beautiful fur, ocelots have long been hunted by man.

28

DANGEROUS BEAUTY

For a cat, great beauty can bring grave danger. Majestic and beautiful cats like the jaguar and ocelot have always been hunted for their fur. It is now illegal in most countries to kill wild cats. But "poachers," illegal hunters, still do.

Cheetahs

▲ The Asiatic lion once roamed a wide area of the Middle East and India. Today, only a few still exist, living on one small game preserve in India.

Jaguars

HABITAT HUNGRY

Animals are dying because cities, villages, and farms are taking up more of their habitats, the natural surroundings they depend on for food and shelter. Meat-eaters, like the mother cheetah who has to feed hungry cubs, must wander for miles looking for prey. As her territory decreases, the chances of survival for her *and* her cubs grow slimmer.

Living high in the mountains of ▶ Central Asia, the snow leopard is still hunted for its thick fur coat.

THREATENED

Once, cougars were common in the western United States. But because they threatened cattle and sheep, many were killed. Now only a few thousand remain, and they are officially listed as a "threatened," though not yet endangered, species.

A cougar sub-species, the Florida panther, inhabits the Florida Everglades and is very endangered. Less than 100 remain.

29

Hollydale Grade School
Gresham, Oregon